Blake's **GO** GUIDES

BETTER
COMMUNICATION
WITH FAMILY, FRIENDS
AND COLLEAGUES

Wendy Beckett

T0348323

PASCAL
PRESS

Copyright © Pascal Press 2005

ISBN 1 74125 147 8

Pascal Press
PO Box 250
Glebe NSW 2037
(02) 8585 4044
www.pascalpress.com.au

Publisher: Vivienne Petris Joannou
Series editor: Ian Rohr
Editor: Jo Avigdor
Page design, layout and cover by *Diʄign*
Photos by Photos.com and Photodisc
Printed in Australia by Printing Creations

A NOTE FROM THE PUBLISHER

The ability to communicate well, to have others understand what we really mean, is a skill. But it is a skill we all can learn or improve on. This Go Guide aims to help you improve your communication skills by building on your strengths and recognising your weaknesses. By following the advice in this Guide you'll soon find that your family, friends and work colleagues are all 'hearing you' when it comes to communication.

As with all our Go Guides we aim to bring you the most useful information in the least number of pages – who has time to read lengthy books? This book will give you quick access to the information, ideas and skills you need to know without the padding contained in so many self-help books.

If you have any comments on how this book could be improved, please do not hesitate to email me at matthew@pascalpress.com.au.

Matthew Blake
Publisher

ABOUT THE AUTHOR

Wendy Beckett has qualifications in psychology, counselling and psychotherapy and has worked extensively in the area of 'conflict resolution'.

Wendy writes about psychological and communication skills in a way that can be easily understood by everyone. Her approach cuts through the jargon and offers straightforward solutions.

Wendy also authored *Quitting Smoking for Life* in the Blake's Go Guide series.

TABLE OF CONTENTS

Communication styles – cultural, family and workplace influences.
The family you were born into, where you live and where you work can all
affect how you communicate with others.

Styles of communication differ markedly from culture to culture and family
to family. Find out what style you use.

Active listening is an essential skill for interacting successfully with others
– but it doesn't come naturally.

Asking questions demonstrates to others that we are interested in them.
Find out how you can draw people out by asking the right questions.

How do you know you have understood what others have said? Learn to
listen accurately and people will respond more positively to you.

Do you sit on the edge of your seat waiting for someone to finish their story
so you can speak? Control this impulse so that others will feel heard.

Respecting personal boundaries means respecting another person's rights
as an individual. Find out what happens if you fail to do this.

Interactions with your family members, friends and colleagues are
enhanced when you acknowledge them. Some common communication
faux pas are also looked at.

Each individual communicates in everyday life in a unique way. So why do
we judge others harshly because they are different to us?

Are you a raver? Perhaps you are frustrated teacher or a control freak?
Check to see which negative communication style describes the way you
behave in company. Adopt a positive style by becoming self aware.

Learn the skills required to deal with conflict in your relationships and
remain positive.

INTRODUCTION

Many of us experience **relationship problems at work, in the home and with our friends**. Too often we blame others for the failure and disappointment we experience. We forget that we too play a role in the health of the relationship. **Our responses to other people are a major factor** in our relationships and we need to own that responsibility.

Everyone who can talk believes that they are a good communicator yet many of us **lack the skills that make for good relationships**. For example, you may have been **influenced by your family** to think that your way of doing or saying things is the 'right way'. As adults, we need to realise that the communication skills that we were given by our families may have been inadequate. The proof is in how well we get along with other people and how well other people get along with us.

How we learned to communicate is **long forgotten** (we may have just mimicked our parents). It doesn't matter how we acquired (or failed to acquire) our communication skills. What does matter is our **ability to recognise** which skills we lack and our **willingness to change**.

Communication is the lifeblood of good relationships. Fortunately the skills required are within the reach of everyone. After all, we learned to talk! Why not learn to communicate better and get **the best out of all our relationships**?

Communicating with another is one of **the most difficult skills** we will ever learn. Partly this is because **we all think we are good at it already** and most of us aren't. We may think that we speak well; that we are well educated; well travelled; experienced in dealing with people; gifted with a large vocabulary; that we are comfortable in conflict or possess any one of a host of other qualities. **What if we had to acknowledge that perhaps we don't communicate as well as we think we do**?

Communication is said to be the **key to having better relationships** but what does that mean? Often people think communication refers to **ease in talking** or the way in which we express ourselves to others. In fact, communication involves a **whole array of skills** which we will be discussing in this Guide.

Few people are good all-round communicators or proficient in the full range of communication skills. Nevertheless, most people you know are very good at one or more of these communication skills. They may be a good listener, an inclusive storyteller, empathetic, easy to talk to, patient, generous, good at bringing people out of themselves, optimistic, or someone with a wise perspective in times of adversity.

Just imagine what the world would be like if we all possessed excellent communication skills!

COMMUNICATION STYLES – CULTURAL, FAMILY AND WORKPLACE INFLUENCES

Cultural influences

Different **communication styles** are in evidence across all cultures and vary in terms of **values, morals, ethics, work ethics, sense of community** and **family view**.

Certain cultures seem to embody some of the communication **skills we would like to possess** – and some we might not. For example, in some societies it is important that guests are supplied with an abundance of food and drink. Excessive generosity is not only the most important consideration, it is a strict requirement. This communicates to the guest that **they are welcome** and can consider themselves at home.

Some cultures can be especially supportive to the bereaved by dressing in black and adopting a sensitive style of communication. For example, to help the person through their grief, they **listen to them intently without interruption** for extended periods of time. Other cultures have particular rules governing how to address an aged person. The aim is to ensure older people **maintain a positive self image** and continue making a contribution. Yet other cultures believe that when you have a problem, it is best to talk it through in detail – in contrast to those who think you should keep your problems to yourself.

No matter what the communication style, it is usually **based on a belief** that this particular way of communicating is thought to be beneficial both socially and culturally. While this may hold true within a particular culture, it may often prove to be inappropriate outside that culture.

Notwithstanding cultural differences, there are some basic communication skills we could all benefit from exposure to in order to ensure the happiness of our ongoing relationships.

Workplace influences

Differences in communication styles are immediately evident in the workplace. They are usually influenced by a person's position within the company hierarchy, their cultural/social background as well as their individual ethics.

Even office gossip and office politics are based on ground-rules which employees may or may not be aware of. A person's participation in office gossip provides a good indication of their communication style. **Good**

communication is about relating. A person's communication style can only be a negative influence if it blocks the possibility of rapport with others.

Family influences

Most people have learnt how to communicate, verbally and non-verbally, by imitating their parents and by adopting their original family's viewpoint. If your parents (your original role-models) were wonderful communicators who excelled in their relationships then all will be well. Unfortunately, this is not usually the case. Many people are unaware that they have unconsciously adopted a whole way of being in the world – that is, they are relating to others in the **same way as their parents did**. They may even be treating friends as if they were their parents! They may **re-enact a familiar family role** – for example, the helpless younger child.

While it takes courage for a person to acknowledge this might be happening, the rewards of addressing these communication behaviours will become obvious over time. There are many ways we can learn to relate better to others, and by doing so, we become more authentic people.

For better relationships good communication is vital. If you weren't lucky enough to be born into a family rich in communication skills, don't worry. **It is never too late to learn**.

ACTIVE LISTENING SKILLS

You may be wondering why it is necessary to talk about listening. Doesn't listening come naturally as a normal part of life? In fact, **few if any of us are good listeners**.

What is a good listener?

Firstly, a good listener allows the other person to **tell their story without interruption**, giving only brief responses such as 'really' or 'I see'. One shows they are *actively* listening by not only allowing a person to complete what they have to say, but also by **asking questions**. This shows a keen interest in what the other person has just said.

Secondly, a good listener **responds in an active way** – and this does not mean chipping in with a story you have just remembered. **Responding** involves looking at the person, reading their facial reactions and focusing on them.

EXERCISE

a) Ask a friend to speak to you for five minutes about some issue in their life without interrupting or adding anything. You are not to try in any way to fix their problem.

b) After three minutes, provide one-word responses only, preferably picking up a word the other person has used. For example, if the person has just said their friend has made them very angry, you repeat the word 'angry', allowing them to clarify further.

c) For the final two minutes, continue with these brief encouragers only. For example: 'Go on', 'Amazing', 'Really' – anything which encourages the other to tell you more.

Remember: you are not to tell your story, make any suggestions or interrupt.

If you are responding by using single words or nods and facial openness the person **feels they are being heard.** If you are not responding appropriately (by gazing off into the distance or fidgeting) you appear to not be listening. In this case, the person will think you are **indifferent, uninterested, bored and unfriendly.**

Being listened to makes people feel **'acknowledged'**. They will, in turn, be more responsive to you. Intimacy is born of being listened to. Its importance cannot be underestimated.

A person who DOES NOT have 'ACTIVE LISTENING SKILLS':

Listens but neglects to remember anything or only part of what you said.

Launches into some other topic entirely after you have finished speaking, failing to acknowledge your topic altogether.

Provides no eye-contact and has no facial expression.

Is physically uneasy: fidgeting, moving around, doing something else or turning away all of which shows their disinterest.

Steals your story from you by talking at length about an apparently related topic without addressing the topic you raised first.

Talks over the top of you when you are speaking.

Acts defensively and negatively whenever someone else speaks because they think they are losing power or being lectured at.

Remains silent and appears to be 'lost in space', adding nothing when you have finished speaking.

States that: 'I've heard all this before', thereby closing down the conversation.

Always behaves in a contrary or competitive manner no matter what topic is under discussion.

Always tops your story by highlighting their own.

Attempts to control the conversation to suit themselves.

Talks incessantly, never giving you the opportunity to join in.

The communication skill of 'active listening' involves more than just plain old listening. It is an **active form of listening** which is quite sophisticated and a great asset to have at your disposal. So, if a person says that you 'never listen to me' you will know you are in need of 'active listening' skills.

QUESTIONING SKILLS

Asking questions demonstrates to others that we are **interested in them and what they have to say** and that we are eager to get to know them. If we can share a conversation and avoid getting locked into solo playing either **listener or talker roles**, then we are making progress.

Most people who have talked during an encounter with someone else will regard the exchange as successful. There is an underlying responsibility in relationships with others to be both a listener and a talker. How much one talks or listens is not as important as having a sense that a 'ball was bounced on both sides of the court'. Otherwise the encounter has amounted to little more than a lecture.

Questions help to draw a person out and clarify their ideas. It helps others feel we are **'with them'**, emotionally and intellectually – not just lost in our own world or concerns. It can be therapeutic to enter another person's world.

Questions can be open-ended or closed. A **closed question** invites a **'yes' or 'no'** answer or a **single word response** – for example, 'What is your favourite sport?' or 'Did you like that film?' are both closed questions. They leave no scope for elaboration. **Open questions** would be: "What do you do in your spare time?' or 'What was it about the film that most interested you?' The open question **invites elaboration**.

EXERCISE

Pause for a moment and consider whether you usually ask open or closed questions when you are with friends. With a friend, practise asking both types of questions and see where it leads.

A person who LACKS THE 'QUESTIONING SKILL':

Only asks questions inviting a yes/no response so you can't elaborate.

Fails to show any curiosity when meeting people for the first time (or even old friends) by rarely asking questions.

Asks too many questions in rapid fire succession ultimately exhausting others.

Shows no facial expression or interest which might encourage you to talk or share a joke.

Doesn't encourage you to continue speaking.

Tends to talk on without stopping to ask for your opinion or ideas.

Asks questions but doesn't wait for the answer!

REFLECTING CONTENT AND EMOTIONS

Reflecting content skill

This skill appears to be fairly straightforward: a person tells you their story then you 'reflect back' by **summarising what they have just said.** All too frequently you will **not** have completely understood what they have said. You then check back with them until you can (in your own words) **accurately reflect their meaning** back to them. While this may sound easy, it is **a rarely practised skill** and one of the **biggest causes of conflict** among couples.

Couples, or people who live together, are often **the worst offenders** because they are convinced that they **know the person so well** that they believe they have understood what was said. Sometimes they have merely second-guessed or else **put their own slant** on what they have heard.

EXERCISE

Ask a friend to speak to you on some topic of interest. When they have finished, reflect back in your own words what you have heard. Observe how many corrections need to be made to content, attitude or meaning.

Now swap places. Do not be kind in this exercise. If they haven't heard you correctly, make them continue reflecting back until you are satisfied that they have 'got it'.

Reflecting emotions skill

This skill is fundamental. It involves empathy – an understanding of how another person is feeling. Failure to show empathy usually results in conflict, rejection and even hatred.

The person who **disregards another's emotions** does so at their peril. Most people will fight for their own integrity. By not 'hearing' and responding to **intensely felt emotions** in others (i.e. bereavement, depression) you show a **lack of caring and humanity.** This is not the same thing as making oneself 'overly responsible for another'; rather it is about **recognising that another person is in difficulty** and letting them communicate that to you.

A common example of **'not reflecting emotions'** is when someone has recently experienced the death of a family member or close friend and the other person keeps talking about their own bereavement experiences of long ago. They fail to recognise that the bereaved person is 'suffering' and in a **'needy state'.** They don't want to hear about your old trouble. Let them have the floor. Show your empathy by listening and accurately reflecting back to them their feelings (i.e. 'You must be feeling so angry'). **Stay with them and their emotions**.

By repeating back to them what they are saying or feeling they will **know you have heard them** and that they are not going mad (a common fear of the recently bereaved).

To reflect emotion means to stay emotionally present with the person. At the same time one needs to **respect their separateness and the uniqueness of their response**. It is not your emotional response that counts – it is theirs. They are **entitled to feel and to act** in whatever way they want. It isn't for you to tell others what their feelings should be nor how they should react.

Denying emotion in another person only **causes it to escalate**. Allow them to express their feelings. **Acknowledging another's pain** and showing empathy to someone in need is making a gift of your time and energy. One day the boot will be on the other foot!

EXERCISE

Ask a friend to recount a story in which their emotions were heightened. Then reflect back in your own words what you have heard and note the corrections to 'emotions' or attitude or meaning. Then swap places. If your friend hasn't understood your feelings correctly, persist until you are satisfied that they have 'got it'.

A person who LACKS THE 'REFLECTING' SKILLS:

Appears disinterested and unfriendly to others.

Runs off half-cocked with information because they have failed to listen properly.

Experiences many conflicts and misunderstandings in their lives.

Claims to be bored by others but really lacks understanding of others.

Finds that people often have to repeat themselves because they haven't felt listened to, acknowledged or understood.

Appears to others to be lacking in empathy.

Avoids emotional involvement and has difficulty getting close to others.

Appears to be self-absorbed and cold. It is impossible to sense any rapport with them.

Behaves with insensitivity and frequently makes callous, offhand comments without thinking first.

Has few close friends or frequently falls out with friends, accusing them of being at fault.

EDITING YOURSELF

This is a skill we all struggle with. Self-editing occurs when you ask yourself 'Should I tell this story now or can it wait until the other person has finished telling their story? **Do I need to tell this story at all**? Does the other person really need to hear it right now? Can it wait until a later time? Is it a good time to tell this? Are they in a listening mood today?'

It is not a good idea to stop another telling their story so you can tell yours **unless it adds something to the proceedings**.

A lot of people sit on the edge of their chair waiting for someone else to finish their story **so they can tell theirs**. Sometimes they are so anxious to tell their story that **they can't hear** the other person at all. This isn't necessarily their fault. A person's memory is often triggered during a conversation and they **remember something similar** which happened to them. **We are all self-referential**. While others can learn from our experiences, timing is important. You don't need to share every thought that comes into your head.

When the person talking is 'venting' they can sometimes forget their audience altogether. If you can't get a word in, **put your hand up and stop them**. You don't have to put up with someone continually **'thinking aloud'** in your face!

EXERCISE

Think over your recent exchanges with others.

◆ Who did most of the talking? Who does most of the talking in your friendships, work relationships, family encounters?
◆ Do you ask others about their weekend experiences? Do you ask them anything about their interests?
◆ Have you ever edited yourself in a conversation or do you give vent to all your 'free flowing' thoughts? Do you just think out loud rather than relate to the person listening to you?

With a friend, discuss a topic (for example, drug use, education, television censorship) and make a point of editing yourself. (You may write down thoughts that you didn't share at the time and then discuss how you felt about this.) Swap over and repeat the exercise.

A person who DOESN'T EDIT THEMSELVES:

Tells stories or anecdotes that take far too long.

Tells unnecessary boring detail, such as the time of day or the date something happened or what they ate for breakfast.

Dominates most conversations so that others find it hard to enter the conversation.

Shares every little thought or experience that pops into their head.

Fails to notice others' uncomfortable body language.

Fails to notice that the other person hasn't spoken.

Makes offhand comments that hurt others and remains completely oblivious.

Frequently talks about their own experiences whenever someone else is speaking.

Is not really 'present' in conversation. They appear lost in an interior monologue, forgetting their audience altogether.

Appears insensitive, boring and overbearing.

RESPECTING PERSONAL BOUNDARIES

A boundary is the **line where you end and another person begins.** Respecting personal boundaries involves recognising and respecting that people are separate and different and exist independently of us and our own wants and needs. They have a right to self-determination.

Respect for boundaries is learnt in our 'family of origin' (i.e. the family we grew up in). For example, if privacy was not a family value in your house, you may not think privacy matters very much. You might then mistakenly assume that privacy doesn't matter to anyone else! You may even think people have no right to privacy. The fact remains, if another person needs privacy and you do not – **you need to respect their need.** You can only decide **what it is right for you** and not what is right for another person.

A family that **models boundaries well** is **respectful of individual differences** and honours people's right to **'control their own life'.** They know it is just as important to look after yourself as it is to look after another person. **They understand fairness.** Family members do not self-sacrifice. They do not bully. They do not put themselves down nor elevate themselves above others. **They do not put others down** by trying to control them or criticising them. They demonstrate mutual respect.

A person who fails to respect ANOTHER PERSON'S BOUNDARIES will:

Keep pushing after you have said 'no'.

Badger a former spouse or partner, abusing them psychologically or physically. They may even be violent.

Act in a domineering way.

Frequently be critical of others.

Unfairly put themselves first in everything and disregard others' needs.

Nag another into giving them what they want.

Force or cajole another into following their personal interests.

Manipulate others and boss other people around.

Act in a controlling manner.

Belittle another for their thoughts or actions.

A person who fails to respect THEIR OWN BOUNDARIES will:

Frequently put themselves last in relation to others.

Be unable to say 'no'.

Take on too much responsibility for others.

Allow themselves to be nagged into doing something they don't want.

Give too much emotionally or financially to others with little thought for their own needs and priorities.

Often have low self-esteem.

ACKNOWLEDGING OTHERS

What is acknowledgement? It is when we feel **listened to and understood.** If you employ all the skills discussed so far then the people around you **will feel acknowledged.**

For example, people **want to make a contribution,** which means **verbalising and communicating their thoughts and feelings.** People also want their efforts to be rewarded by **a sense of connection** with whomever they are interacting. Acknowledgment (or lack of it) is usually **modelled within the family of origin.**

People who have **never received much acknowledgement in childhood** tend not to give it, often saying they 'feel silly' acknowledging people around them. Praising others is actually quite hard for such a person but **with practice** this skill can flourish, particularly in the workplace. The end result is that people will feel a lot better about projects they are working on and work relations will be enhanced.

A person who FAILS TO ACKNOWLEDGE OTHERS will:

Repeatedly forget to thank someone and then justify their position by claiming it is unimportant.

Rarely, if ever, give praise (outside their own family) and justify their position by being negative about others whom they imagine are 'demanding' it of them.

Often consciously or unconsciously solicit for praise and acknowledgement themselves.

Fail to recognise that someone has put themselves out for them.

Be frustrating to work with and seem laconic, uninterested and unfriendly.

Be hard to 'read' on the basis of their words or their body language (they are often poker-faced.)

Create low morale at work.

EXERCISE

The following is a useful exercise for getting started on your new communication skills:

1. Set a stop watch to go off every two minutes over a period of eight minutes.
2. Ask a friend to tell you a problem and then every two minutes employ your new communication skills.
3. For the first two minutes you must only listen.

4. For the next two minutes, only use brief or one-word encouragers (i.e. 'Yes', 'Really', 'What then?')
5. For the next two minutes ask **open** or **closed** questions (remember, the latter are questions that will receive a yes/no or short answer).
6. For the last two minutes reflect back the content of what the other person has said as well as their feelings (i.e. summarising what they have said).
7. Swap places and then discuss.

Common faux pas in communication

Are you guilty of any of the following scenarios?

Topping someone else's story!

In your family: *Your brother is talking excitedly about the high-school art prize he has just won. You talk over the top of him, telling everyone in the room how you won the best art prize for New South Wales in 1982, depriving him of his moment of triumph.*

If you had used **better communication skills** you would have shown genuine interest by asking him a series of increasingly specific questions about his painting and listened to his responses. Communicating your pleasure in his success will be evidence of your supportive attitude and will lead to a positive connection between you both. The example you set of modelling a positive approach will very likely be reciprocated in the future.

With friends: *A friend hardly gets through telling you about her adventurous outing when you cut across her with a similar story of your own. In this instance you are wanting (perhaps unconsciously) for **your story** to be heard. You are ignoring her story altogether.*

If you had used **better communication skills** you would have pulled back from telling your story until after due attention had been paid to your friend's story. Say something that shows you have heard and appreciated what she has recounted. Let her hear and see your physical or verbal response to what she is telling you. How else can she know that you have taken in what she has just said?

With work colleagues: *In a staff meeting, a colleague undermines the efforts you made in a recent promotion campaign by interrupting you when you are explaining how you achieved your recent success.*

If you had used **better communication skills** you would have called for a temporary halt to the meeting and asked that each salesperson be allowed the courtesy of reporting their story uninterrupted. Simple but effective. An alternative response could be: 'Thank you Joe for your comments. Now I would like to complete my presentation uninterrupted and I'll invite questions at the end'.

Failing to edit yourself

Your memory has been jogged by something your friend has just said and you are dying to tell your story while they are still speaking. So you interrupt and start talking yourself.

Ask yourself: 'How is my friend feeling now? Would this person find my story interesting? Is now a good time to tell this story or could it wait? Perhaps the other person still has something to add to their story. Perhaps they want a response from me!'

Communication involves sharing. You need to consider whether you are riding roughshod over the other person by talking them into a state of submission. Are they being forced into being your captive audience?

If you want to talk endlessly and be listened to, **you are being unfair.** One-sided conversation soon gets boring for any listener no matter how polite they are to you. Everyone wants to join in and **have a turn** – not just listen to you. In short, the listener may actually start to feel abused and will most likely start to regard you as selfish and tiresome.

Remember: like a kaleidoscope, ideas light up in your brain once you are triggered to remember something. However, you don't have to relate to another person every thought or story that comes into your head. Show some interest in the other person's memories or stories and they may in turn show interest in yours.

Failing to ask questions

*You are in company with friends. You listen to what they have to say and make a few remarks yourself **without asking them any questions.***

Communication is about mutual discovery. Communication is about exchange and getting to know another person and how they think and feel.

Ask yourself: 'If I **never ask** questions, will this person think I am uninterested in them?'

Remember: show some curiosity. People are not in existence merely for you to toss your words, interests, ideas and stories at. They have some of their own. Draw them out. Ask several questions. Try to find out what the topic in question means to them. After all, they have chosen to introduce a particular topic for a reason. You may find that they, in turn, become a responsive listener to you.

Failing to read people's faces and body language

You are talking to a friend and fail to notice that they haven't spoken for most of the time you have been together. They seem distracted and unhappy but you carry on regardless.

Ask yourself: 'What is the response of the person I am talking to? Are they agitated? Do they look frustrated? What is their facial expression?'

Communication involves body language. A person's body language and facial expression is as much a part of the exchange as words.

Remember: just because you feel like talking, it doesn't mean the other person feels the same way at that particular moment.

Being contrary

Your friend expresses an opinion and you immediately feel the impulse to make an opposing statement.

Ask yourself: 'Does this person really enjoy being contradicted every time they open their mouth?' 'If I continually do this, am I going to make more enemies than friends?'

Communication is not a competition – turning it into one only demonstrates how insecure you are about your own intellect. Your need to keep 'antler-bashing' people into submission will soon become very obvious to others. At best, you'll come across as a highly disagreeable person.

Remember: when someone raises a topic it is not a flag of war – it is just a topic they may be interested in exploring with you. Conversation does not always have to trigger you into conflict. You are missing out on one of life's great pleasures if you are always turning every exchange into a war zone. Most have learnt this pattern of relating in childhood but it can be overcome.

Talking over others and finishing their sentences

Your friend has just started to talk about something and you start to talk over the top of them while they are still speaking. Soon you jump in and finish their sentences for them.

Ask yourself: 'What's the hurry? Am I doing this so that I can hurry things along and **get to tell my story**?'

Communication is not a race. Some people may feel you are being too impatient with them. Relax and enjoy a leisurely interchange.

Remember: we all relate at different speeds and this is part of our unique difference. It's better to wait!

Dominating the conversation when visiting relatives

You are surrounded by relatives so you give yourself permission to be the centre of attention by dominating the conversation. You only talk about family matters and ignore some visitors who have recently arrived.

Ask yourself: 'Is your news the only point of interest? Are your stories the only ones in existence?' Stop and consider the other people present. Ask them questions.

Communication isn't just about your family. If there are other people present, include them in the conversation. Many a visitor is left feeling bored and excluded by family talk.

Remember: family often causes people to slip back into bad old communication habits.

Remaining silent and making others do all the work

You are visiting family or friends and fall into the familiar role of staying silent because you don't feel like talking. Stay home if you feel like solitude!

Communication is an exchange. To exclude yourself from social responsibility by leaving it up to the others to always make social occasions work is just laziness.

Ask yourself: 'Am I the silent type? If so, why? What is it about being with others that causes me distress or indifference?'

Remember: if you don't feel like company, stay home. At best you will be regarded as boring, indifferent and selfish. You may end up suffering a lot of loneliness in your life. Before you visit someone think about what topics might be of interest to you both. If you find it hard to be with others, begin by limiting the time you spend with people and then gradually increase the duration.

Associate with people who have good social skills and copy them. With practice you will develop skills of your own and you can then build on these. When going to a social event tell yourself there is bound to be one person whose company I will enjoy. Who knows? Perhaps a new friendship will be born!

Judging people negatively

Your friend introduces you to her aunt from interstate. You take an immediate dislike to her because you don't like her taste in clothes and she doesn't say much.

Ask yourself: 'Is this person shy?' 'Perhaps she is distracted by some problem?' 'Does a person's taste in clothes indicate their real character?'

Communication is an opportunity to get to know someone. Drawing a person out in conversation allows you to get to know them better rather than relying on superficial impressions.

Remember: give others a break. We all have bad days and we all relate differently. If you adopt a negative attitude to others on first meeting them it will colour the event in a negative way. Most people are a little uncomfortable when meeting strangers. But a stranger could become a friend later.

The other person may be struggling just as much as you with an awkward encounter so relax. If in doubt, show some interest in them and get the ball rolling. Most, if not all people, enjoy talking about themselves and their interests.

An interesting person is someone who finds other people interesting!

Knocking down other people's ideas

You are discussing possible solutions to a problem with colleagues at work. However, whenever someone comes up with a suggestion you immediately declare that it will never work.

Communication involves testing new ideas with others. I'll bet others don't see you as all-knowing. Share ideas and resist cutting off communication possibilities.

Ask yourself: 'Am I really insecure? Am I just trying to *appear* confident? Do I really believe I know more than other people?'

Remember: if your first response to a suggestion is always a negative one, think again. It is better to go with an idea first and see where it takes you rather than cut it down instantly. The impulse to be negative and always see the flaws in something says more about you than the topic at hand.

INDIVIDUAL COMMUNICATION STYLES

Most people are willing to concede that individuals **experience and process bereavement in different ways** and will exercise patience and understanding at such times. Yet it is not commonly acknowledged that the way in which each individual person communicates **in everyday life** is also different. A simple example might be that under pressure, some people talk their heads off while others remain silent. This is a **communication difference**.

Communication styles can vary significantly in how a person talks, how they behave and how they react to others – the differences are endless. Often we **judge others** on these differences. This judgement is often bound up with feeling uncomfortable around someone who is different from us and it is usually negative. We judge others negatively because we cannot understand their behaviour or responses to everyday events. We may assume that behaviour and **communication patterns** are universal and set in stone.

This view is not the result of arrogance, but rather is born out of **a false belief** that we are all raised in exactly the same way **with the same values** in the same community. If people deviate from our own norms we judge them harshly.

Some might attribute this to **a form of social Darwinism** – the belief that the survival of a species is dependent upon every one of its members adhering to the **same set of rules** in all circumstances. On reflection we know this is not true – and yet still we complain. Why? Because we **feel threatened, annoyed, and aggravated** by a person who does not behave or speak as we ourselves do. This is perhaps the hardest human lesson – to accept difference.

In psychology there is a saying: '**Everyone is doing the best that they can**'. Look at it from the **point of view of the 'other person'**. They are seeing the world or their situation through their own eyes, and interpreting it on the basis of their **own individual background and experiences** – one cannot expect otherwise. They are, in fact, doing the best that they can, the best they know how, given who they are. In a sense, knowing this should make it easier to **forgive bad communication or behaviour.** (This doesn't mean one shouldn't be self protective and reject bad behaviour. However, it does mean we can operate with 'enlightened understanding'.)

NEGATIVE AND POSITIVE COMMUNICATION STYLES

Some examples of negative styles

The know-all

The **know-all** can't wait to let you how much **more they know than you** about every topic you raise or discuss. The know-all isn't prepared to listen to others and is always **seeking to out-manoeuvre** them with their superior knowledge. The know-all is insecure, but rather than be shown up they will **hijack the conversation** by verbal fencing.

The control freak

The **control freak** can't wait to tell other people what to do, how to do it and how to think. They come across as **highly critical**. No-one likes to feel incompetent and the control freak is extremely fearful of this themselves. They constantly put others down, verbally overriding them and **trying to dominate** with their own ideas and plans.

Their behaviour is aggressive, which **alienates those around them.** By always **'taking over'** the other person they are implying that they are too hopelessly incompetent to act or think for themselves. They fail to give the other person credit for being **able to make their own decisions** nor do they respect the fact that others **may do things differently.**

Control freaks make others around them angry, frustrated, depressed and negative. It is the surest way to **lose friends or scare people away.** The control freak is always anxious underneath because their quest for control is ultimately impossible to achieve. They are overly watchful of the actions and behaviours of those around them. They need to learn **to live and let live**.

The agree-er

The **agree-er** always **goes along with the views or desires of others**. They never protest. They don't defend themselves but rather apologise for themselves. They **avoid conflict** of any sort and want only harmony wherever they go. They don't want to stand out.

They never want to be confronted and therefore let the wishes of others **dominate their lives.** While they have thoughts and feelings just like everyone else, they rarely show them. While they may be praised for being so 'easygoing', others may take the opportunity to take advantage of them. Friends may grow disrespectful knowing that the agree-er **will not fight back.**

For the agree-er, conflict equals **loss, fear and anxiety**. Their hidden worry is to be rejected as unworthy. This may be rooted in childhood experiences of parental conflict when they feared a parent might leave home.

The agree-er **needs to examine their fears** and realise that confrontations do not necessarily have to result in negative or threatening consequences. **Conflict may even be positive** in that it can clear up misunderstandings quickly. Being disagreeable **sometimes** is a natural part of being human.

The didactic

The **didactic** (or **detailer)** is like a frustrated teacher. When talking, they **go into great detail** so that the other person will learn as much as is humanly possible about the subject under discussion. They of course, remain the **fountain of all knowledge**. They always give out far more information than is needed.

A common example may be a computer consultant who goes into unnecessary details rather than focus on what the client actually wants to know. Such a person is **unaware of their audience.** They **fail to read the face, voice or expression** of the person on the receiving end of these unwanted lessons. They are the teacher and you, therefore, must be the **willing student.**

Often they **insult people's intelligence** with their explanations because they **assume zero knowledge** in the person they are talking to. The listener may even have the information already but doesn't get the opportunity to say so.

The didactic one can often come across **as authoritarian**, which puts people off. They are often too blind to see that others are annoyed or bored with them. Their actions **mask a fear** of not being **educated enough** to compete or not **interesting enough** to attract friends.

The contrarian

The **contrarian** is a person who, no matter what is said, will **loudly state an opposing view.** Since they are not interested in extending their knowledge or exploring a topic fully there can be **no journey of discovery** or discussion of ideas; rather they are **contemptuous of most people** and want to **force their ideas on others.** This is dominating behaviour. Often the views they spout may not be genuinely held by them but every conversation **seems to impel them** to take an opposing stand.

The **contrarian** is fearful of not winning **an imagined contest.** They play devil's advocate to be one step ahead of their imagined opponent. In reality they **crave a sense of superiority.** Their insecurity drives them to gain a victory rather than focus on the topic at hand.

There is a **lack of generosity** in denying others the pleasure of knowing something, of being 'right' or contributing something new. Contrarians usually lack really deep friendships. They need to **work on their self-worth** and learn to temper this annoying habit; only then can they **appreciate the worth of others**.

The raver

The **raver** uses up all the talking space. They are **continually overexcited** and have **not learnt to edit themselves**. They are domineering and exhausting to be with. Ravers appear to have little interest in how others regard them. While any dialogue between people can be uneven at times, it should **always be an exchange**. Because a raver never leaves 'a break in the traffic', it's hard for others to jump in and make a contribution.

Ravers act the way they do because they are nervous and excitable or because they have **never learnt how to share a conversation**. They are oblivious to the responses of others. They need to read people's faces and 'check in' with those listening to them. Ravers need to consider their audience more and **self-edit**.

The incessant questioner

The **incessant questioner** asks endless questions, **letting others do all the work** in social interactions. They can leave others feeling drained and wondering whether they even care about the answers being given.

Incessant questioners **never consider the reactions of others**. They are fearful of not being taken seriously intellectually and may be **extremely nervous**. They are often **socially inexperienced** insofar as they have not learnt 'how to share a conversation'.

Incessant questioners give the impression that they **want the facts and they want them quickly** so that they can leave. Usually they are overly worried about social interactions and **this fear** triggers further questioning. They want to be liked and imagine that asking people constant questions will equate with relating – instead it ends up being **an inquisition**.

The comedian

The comedian makes a joke out of everything, managing to turn everyone's **attention towards themselves**. This may be fine in a social setting but it is annoying in a work situation which requires people to focus on the issue at hand. They can waste large amounts of time, all because they **need to be liked a lot**.

Their behaviour is usually aimed at **covering up their fears** – perhaps a fear of social situations. They believe everyone *must* have a good time, and worry that they don't contribute enough. This in turn leads to **overdoing it socially with humour**. They believe they have found a **sure-fire way to be popular**.

The comedian is often **lonely or depressed in private**, adopting a public role that they cannot live up to as frequently as they would like. While they were probably **praised as children** for their comic skills, it becomes a burden because not all situations are funny. They are limited in thinking there is **only one role in life for them**.

The intense person

The **intense person** claims they only want to **connect deeply** when in fact they are really trying to **control the social situation** on the basis of self-interest. **They crave intimacy**. Others may prefer a light exchange and feel 'pushed' into having a **'deep and meaningful'** interaction when they don't want it.

Whose needs are really being met here? The intense person **confuses intimacy with friendship**. The only way they know how to get close to people is by being overly personal or intense. Since p**ersonal boundaries are blurred** in the intense person, they fail to respect **the needs, privacy and feelings of others**.

Self-revelation is a choice, not something one should be forced or tricked into by a stranger. Intense people can frequently make others feel unsafe. Those at the receiving end of their gaze **may experience a feeling of violation** or be angered by a conversation they have been forced into against their wishes. The intense person is dominant and needs to consider other people more and make an effort to 'read' them. They need to be **less self-focused**.

Negative communication styles – underlying causes

You will notice from the above descriptions that most people with negative communication styles are **utterly unaware of the impact they are having on others** or else they would desist. There is also a **power issue** involved and social dominance is all too frequently the goal.

Lack of social and communication skills is generally to blame. A person's **role in their original family** might also be a factor. For example, the youngest may have been spoilt and their bad behaviour indulged. When, as an adult, they cannot display thoughtless or dependent behaviour in a friendship or work situation, they wrongly blame everyone around them. Equally, an elder child may, as an adult, block others' independence by always 'taking over'. We all have **traces of some or all of these habits**

within us. But to be locked into one type of behaviour suggests the need to **become more adaptable**.

Positive communication styles
Self-awareness and good communication skills

Achieving a positive communication style requires us to step back and take a **critical look at ourselves**. We need to ask 'Could I be preventing people from getting along better with me?' Self-awareness is a prerequisite for good communication with others.

In general, good communicators know how to start a conversation, join in a social situation, end a social situation, leave an unsatisfactory situation, and remain in control when in a difficult situation. They **employ all the communication skills**, including reflecting, self-editing, acknowledging and respecting personal boundaries.

Good communicators stand out in a social setting and are **often popular**. They can be **either extroverts or introverts**. They are people adept at communicating in a **productive and positive way** with others. Because of this skill they often get most of the things they want in life.

Use of praise

Yet another positive communication skill used by good communicators is praise. **Praise is always under-rated** and yet it is one of the most effective precursors to good communication. It lets the other person know you are **positively predisposed** to them. It places them at ease and **increases their confidence**.

Some people will say they are **uncomfortable praising others** – or even that it feels false. It is likely that they themselves have an issue about praise and were probably **never praised themselves** when growing up.

We learn the benefits of praise every time someone praises us. Why not pass on this happy experience to others? It could become a permanent part of your new way of responding to others – a positive way.

To withhold praise when it is due is a sure way to **negate the value of another person** – virtually rendering their contribution worthless. Why not break the cycle? Praise one person a day no matter how insignificant the reason. Then praise three people in the same day. Alternatively, praise someone close to you three times a day and watch the effect. Try it and you may be surprised. Praising others seems to make most humans feel positive about themselves as well as other people.

RESOLVING CONFLICT

Cause of pain and angst

Most people associate conflict with its **destructiveness:** anger, anxiety, fear, aggression, distress and unhappiness. (Violence is a separate issue, being an extreme reaction to conflict.) Ordinary, day-to-day conflict is the cause of much pain and angst.

Some people try to avoid conflict or suppress it while others engage in it all too frequently. **There is another way.** We need to learn the **skills required to deal with conflict** in our relationships and remain positive.

Conflict can result in war, stalemate or resolution, the latter being the **ideal outcome** for everyone concerned.

Gender differences in resolving conflict

For many reasons there are **differences in how men and women resolve** conflict; mostly these are culturally determined or inculcated through social norms. All too frequently it remains socially unacceptable for a woman to display anger.

For example, in displaying **assertive qualities**, women can find themselves rejected by both men and women alike. The response of anger is much **more easily tolerated in males.**

The male response of being assertive or aggressive is viewed as appropriate and even socially acceptable. Men may imagine that it is right and fitting for their decisions to take precedence.

It is crucial that each gender be given **due acknowledgement** in regard to their **different approaches to conflict.** What is the point of speaking French to a German speaker? It only wastes time. The mere assertion of will is unlikely to result in a satisfactory outcome to conflict. It will only send it underground, to resurface at another time – perhaps even more **loaded with resentment**. If adequate acknowledgement is not given to the other's point of view then the **problem will remain.**

While not all men or women fit into **a particular stereotype** of behaviour it is helpful to consider the following generalisations on '**common gender differences**':

Common GENDER DIFFERENCES in resolving conflict

Men	Women
Facts are important and they tend to emphasise facts first.	Feelings are important and they will usually assert feelings first.
Claim to be reality focused.	Perceive a situation via feelings.
Tend to disassociate from the feeling component and deride any suggestion of feelings by another.	Tend to disclose feelings and demand they be taken into account. They may criticise anyone who fails to express feelings.
Focus on problem-solving, often wanting to be the one 'who does the solving'. Prefer to finalise an issue quickly without processing the problem. Focus on one issue.	Focus on the interpersonal relationship underlying the problem. They often talk of changing how they relate to another or how another relates to them.
Discount attempts to broaden the topic under discussion. Talk the language of the present. Dislike past and future references.	Tend to see a problem holistically. Both the past and the future are important.
Focus on the content in front of them.	Focus on the relationship in front of them.
Can be very competitive in their approach to conflict, even aggressive if it means getting their needs met.	Tend to be co-operative and more willing to compromise. They want stable relations between all parties.
Very concerned about losing face, status and position and therefore don't like to admit to mistakes.	Less concerned with status and losing face. See conciliation as progressive.

WHAT IS GOING ON IN CONFLICT SITUATIONS?

The persecutor-victim-rescuer triangle

Common roles that people take up in conflict are that of **victim, persecutor** or **rescuer.**

1. In the **victim role** they claim that the other person has harmed them in some way and they are reacting out of powerlessness. (There are, of course, real victims who have suffered injustice, abuse, accident or loss and this **does not** refer to them.)
2. In the **persecutor role** they are the perpetrator who oppresses the other person relentlessly.
3. In the **rescuer role** they are constantly saving someone from some situation.

Since there is a **power game going on** in most conflicts, many people fall into old familiar **childhood or family roles** when the heat is on. That is, they play the role of victim, persecutor or rescuer. Which role did you play when growing up?

Persecutors: demand obedience; rely on reward and punishment as a strategy; bully and use their position of authority; demean and bulldoze others with their point of view. The message is: **I'm OK. You are not OK.**

Rescuers: assume that others constantly need their support and help; deny their own needs and act like martyrs; feel responsible for solving the problems of others; side with other victims against perceived persecutors. The message is: **I'm OK. You are not OK.**

Victims: feel they are helpless and dependent on others; talk and act as if everyone is against them; act in a defeatist manner; lay blame on others so they can solicit for sympathy; many feel depressed. The message is: **I'm not OK. You are OK.**

Breaking free of roles

To break free of these three roles certain things have to change. **If you change the roles you are playing, others will change their roles as well.** For example, if one person constantly picks on a 'victim' and wins, the bullying will continue. However, if one day the 'victim' changes roles and acts assertively – the game is up and the bullying cannot continue.

What changes could help?

◆ The 'persecutor' needs to become a **consultant.**
◆ The 'rescuer' needs to become a **facilitator.**
◆ The 'victim' needs to become a **responsible person.**

If a persecutor were to become **a consultant** they could:
◆ 'actively' listen and respect the needs of others as well as themselves
◆ share expertise
◆ be 'assertive' rather than aggressive when stating their needs
◆ give constructive rather than critical feedback
◆ share the decision-making.

If a rescuer were to become **a facilitator** they could:
◆ be more objective
◆ encourage others to look after their own needs instead of doing it for them
◆ 'actively' listen
◆ state their own needs and become more assertive
◆ encourage others to listen to each other rather than falling into playing the parent
◆ discuss the likely outcomes if the other person continues in their current behaviour
◆ introduce new strategies to assist others in problem-solving
◆ respect others' ability to find solutions to their own problems in their own way.

If a victim were to become **a responsible person** they could:
◆ exercise their power more and be more actively responsible
◆ locate and seek out information skills and necessary professional assistance
◆ recognise and acknowledge the needs of others
◆ actively listen and assert their personal needs
◆ directly involve themselves in decision-making
◆ participate with others in problem-solving.

Changing roles can turn a situation of conflict into something **entirely manageable.** Each person would become motivated to problem-solve and mutual demands would be reduced, freeing up the situation so a resolution to conflict can be found.

Failure to transform the roles of victim, persecutor and rescuer usually **results in a stalemate** and the painful emotions, resentment, hurt, anger, regret, fear and frustration, remain.

Unproductive conflict strategies include:
- avoidance
- blame
- minimisation
- personal rejection
- force
- manipulation.

Productive conflict strategies include:
- openness
- supportiveness
- equality
- mutual respect
- empathy
- willingness to find a solution than meets at least part of each other's needs.

A WIN/WIN APPROACH TO RESOLVING CONFLICT

Being pro-active

Blaming another for a conflict is **pointless and passive**; it only perpetuates the conflict situation. A win/win approach is a far preferable alternative. While to some, the term 'win/win' may sound like jargon, it is in fact a **highly effective, pro-active method** for resolving conflict.

Originally developed by Cornelius and Faire (1989) the win/win approach has been **adapted and widely used** in all kinds of conflict situations.

Four key steps

There are four steps:

1. Find out what the conflicting parties need to happen and why. (Define the problem.)
2. Find out where the differences dovetail.
3. Explore the options.
4. Work towards cooperation and compromise.

The **key features** of the win/win approach are:

- Ensure all needs have been considered.
- Concentrate on the approach not the outcome.
- Keep focussed – stay with the issue.
- Examine the long-term consequences, the advantages of win/win, and the options.
- Make it easy to say 'yes'.
- Remain fair and respectful to both sides at all times.
- Aim always for co-operation.

The right attitude

Training and management consultant Gilda Dangot-Simpkin (1991) points out that the **attitude** a negotiator takes into a dispute situation **influences the outcome**. It is fundamental to maintaining a positive relationship throughout the conflict resolution process.

Ultimately, the aim should be to build a relationship beyond the negotiation process.

An effective negotiation process

Dangot-Simpkin outlines eight attitudes required for an effective negotiation process.

They are:

1. Consider 'the other' a partner throughout the process at all times.
2. Be willing for both parties to reach their goals.
3. Remain open to more than one perspective during the process.
4. Remain positive to the personality of the others in negotiation.
5. Be adult enough to help the other meet their needs as well as your own.
6. Consider all options and alternatives and allow exploration.
7. Realise and accept that there are multiple ways to achieve the wanted result.
8. Appreciate that negotiation is an ongoing shared process and not about personal victories.

The importance of commitment

It is important to be able to **commit to an agreement** at the end of the negotiations. In the **closing phase** you should be able to:

◆ form agreements
◆ develop an action plan
◆ set a timeframe
◆ put in place a review process.

APPROPRIATE ASSERTIVENESS

All too often people feel **overpowered by the demands and needs of others**. This is unfair. A situation is only fair if you and the person you are in conflict with **both have your needs met** – not just one of you.

Three easy steps for appropriate assertiveness are:
1. State clearly what the problem is.
2. Say 'When you do X I feel Y.'
3. Say 'I would prefer that you a b c ...'

Do not draw breath when you are stating these three things and do not allow yourself to be interrupted. Do not lay blame. Be **simple and to the point** in your language.

If the person doesn't respond to your request, walk away and let them think about it. **Do not argue.** (This will only draw you back into the conflict.)

You have stated your case. You will feel better having done so. The other person's response is theirs and theirs alone. **Do not tolerate abuse**. Leave promptly if they wish to argue. Should they wish to talk, **keep repeating** what you want. Do not waver and do not be tricked into arguing.

At all costs avoid getting yourself into a circular argument. Leave if one starts. Your mind will be free and they will be the one carrying the load now, not you.

You are going to get very good at this with practice!

WHAT IS YOUR COMMUNICATION STYLE?

Now that we have outlined some basic communication skills, find out what **your communication style** is by completing the following quiz.

ANSWER THE FOLLOWING QUESTIONS BY TICKING A BOX.

1. I interrupt people mid-stream in their story to tell my story about the same topic.

   ALWAYS ☐   SOMETIMES ☐   NEVER ☐

2. I ask questions of people when I meet them and try to draw them out.

   ALWAYS ☐   SOMETIMES ☐   NEVER ☐

3. I say whatever comes into my mind.

   ALWAYS ☐   SOMETIMES ☐   NEVER ☐

4. I summarise or repeat back to people what they have told me just to make sure I have understood them properly.

   ALWAYS ☐   SOMETIMES ☐   NEVER ☐

5. I remain silent when people tell me things and don't respond.

   ALWAYS ☐   SOMETIMES ☐   NEVER ☐

6. I genuinely believe I know more about most things than other people.

   ALWAYS ☐   SOMETIMES ☐   NEVER ☐

7. I think most people aren't as good as me in doing practical things.

   ALWAYS ☐   SOMETIMES ☐   NEVER ☐

8. I usually agree with other people to keep the peace.

   ALWAYS ☐   SOMETIMES ☐   NEVER ☐

9. I need other people to like me.

   ALWAYS ☐   SOMETIMES ☐   NEVER ☐

10. I like to educate others by explaining things to them.

    ALWAYS ☐   SOMETIMES ☐   NEVER ☐

11. I frequently disagree with the thinking and views of others.

    ALWAYS ☐   SOMETIMES ☐   NEVER ☐

12. I like to play the devil's advocate regularly.

ALWAYS ☐   SOMETIMES ☐   NEVER ☐

13. I do most of the talking in company.

ALWAYS ☐   SOMETIMES ☐   NEVER ☐

14. I do most of the listening in company.

ALWAYS ☐   SOMETIMES ☐   NEVER ☐

15. I ask people lots of questions when I meet them.

ALWAYS ☐   SOMETIMES ☐   NEVER ☐

16. I need to feel that everyone is happy when I am in their company.

ALWAYS ☐   SOMETIMES ☐   NEVER ☐

17. I want to please people most of the time.

ALWAYS ☐   SOMETIMES ☐   NEVER ☐

18. I don't do small talk.

ALWAYS ☐   SOMETIMES ☐   NEVER ☐

If you answered 'always' or 'sometimes' to most of the first five questions you might need to improve your **listening skills**.

If you answered 'always' or 'sometimes' for most of the remaining questions look again at the section on **communication styles** and see if you can recognise yourself. Only when you become truly aware of your pattern of communication can you begin to try and improve it.

Communication for couples

Some common COMMUNICATION PROBLEMS in families

The male view	The female view
1. Feeling pressured to talk through their wife's/partner's emotional responses.	1. Feeling marooned as the emotionally 'responsible' one in the family.
2. Being criticised for not contributing enough to domestic chores.	2. Senses a lack of intimacy, in her relationship to partner or children.
3. Feeling pressured to discipline the children.	3. Is overly responsible for domestic chores.
4. Criticised by wife/partner for not spending enough 'quality' family time.	4. Doesn't feel heard.
5. Being pressured to engage in activities with family/in-laws/partners/friends.	5. Criticised for nagging, worrying excessively.

Common NEGATIVE RESPONSES in families

Common negative male responses	Common negative female responses:
'I don't like sitting and talking. I don't like getting intense and deep.'	"No-one ever listens to me.'
'I work. It's your job to discipline the children.'	'You never discipline the children. It's always me.'
'I'm not going to your parents for dinner.'	'Why do I always have to be the one to organise social outings?'
'I've got enough on my plate with work.'	'You've left all your stuff lying around. '
'I just want to relax when I come home.'	'You never do anything around the house.'

Common POSITIVE RESPONSES in families	
Common positive male responses	**Common positive female responses**
'Why don't you just sit down and tell me what's bothering you and we'll work on this problem together.'	'I don't need you to fix or solve anything but I feel supported when you hear me out.'
'The problem is about A. When you say B I feel frustrated. I would prefer you do C.'	'The situation is W. When you do X I feel Y. I would prefer you did Z.'
'How can I help in all this?'	'The children are our joint responsibility so how can we manage them together better.'
'How is it for you when C happens?'	'Let's be mates about this and help each other out by listening.'
'Is there a way we can do a better job of this and share responsibility?'	'Is there a better way we can divide the housework between us?'

Communicating better with your spouse/ partner

How can you communicate better to resolve the above?

◆ Choose a time that is **convenient for both** of you. Book that time and limit it to about half an hour or whatever suits. You must both **agree on the amount of time** you are to devote to this problem.

◆ Brush up your **'active listening skills'** and be firm.

◆ Apply the **'appropriate assertiveness'** skill. Avoid statements such as 'you never' or 'you always'. Begin instead with 'I' statements. Remember, no-one has the power to make you feel, think or do anything **unless you give them that power**.

◆ Are you playing the persecutor, the rescuer or the victim? Refer again to the triangle described earlier.

◆ Refer to the section on 'gender differences in resolving conflict'.

◆ Refer to the section on negotiation skills and be mindful that **both parties' needs** *must* be addressed if there is to be a positive result.

Teenagers' relationship with parents

Teenagers are often:

- criticised for being **difficult, rude and disagreeable**
- judged for not being sensible enough or are **not trusted enough** to go out alone.
- judged for wearing unusual clothes, haircuts, jewellery, or **listening to different music.**

They may **feel frustrated** at not being able to **exercise control** over their own lives and sometimes have problems which they feel they **can't talk to anyone about.**

NEGATIVE teenager's response	POSITIVE teenagers response
'No-one ever does anything for me.'	'Can you help me with this?'
'Why am I the one who always has to do everything?'	'Tell me what it is about so and so that worries you where I'm concerned.'
'Get xmp#!'	'Please listen to me first.'
'You never let me do what I want.'	'You can trust me to be sensible. I've shown responsibility already in lots of different ways.'
'I'll wear/do whatever I want to and you can't stop me.'	'Let's meet each other half-way.'

Parents' relationship with their children

Parents often feel:

- **frustrated** by the type of negative response their teenagers give them
- **guilty** about their parenting skills, believing they should know best at all times and yet experience **self-doubt**
- **over-powered** by their children's demands and needs
- **confused** about how to best deal with conflict with their children
- **fearful** that they are losing control over their children
- **anxious** about the direction their children are heading
- that they and their children **compare unfavourably** to others.

NEGATIVE parental response	POSITIVE parental response
'You never do anything I ask you.'	'When you do X I am so pleased with you.'
'You're an idiot, stupid.'	'The thing you are really good at is …'
'I'll never give you X again. You're too careless.'	'Let's meet each other half-way on this problem hey?'
'Get me this, then get me that, now do this, and then do that.'	'Tell me what you are so worried, angry or upset about?'
'Why can't you be like the boy/girl next door? They are nice children.'	'Tell me what's happening with you and together we might be able to work something out.'

Better communication between parents and children can be achieved by:

- Applying **'active listening skills'** and hearing each other out. This will require that the parent and child each have **uninterrupted talk**. (This means only *one* person will speak at a time. A response will only be given after the other has finished saying what they want to say.)
- The adult applying the **'questioning skill'**.
- **Praising** anything positive the child has said or done.
- The parent reflecting back to the child what they have said to ensure they **feel properly heard**.
- Applying **negotiation skills.**
- Giving the child options to make them feel they have **'chosen' to agree** on a particular matter. This also gives them a feeling of personal power.
- **Avoiding the persecutor/victim/rescuer triangle** by finding ways parent and child can move out of these familiar roles.

In-laws and conflict

Since the people involved come from a **different family background**, they will have different values, priorities and responses and this will have an impact in conflict situations among in-laws. **Birth order of the participants** may also be having an effect. (For example, a younger child (now adult) may be used to **others taking responsibility** to sort out their problems. If they are the eldest, they may feel pressured to always act as the **'responsible one'**). It is not unusual for people to **marry or partner** with someone who has similar qualities, both good and bad, to family members.

In-laws sometimes find it hard to accept someone from **outside their family** because they **think and behave differently**. It does not mean they are a bad person – they just do things differently.

Rigid family boundaries

Some families unknowingly develop what is known as **'rigid family boundaries'** in which a belief emerges that **'no-one outside the family can be trusted'**. Sadly this leads to an **unhappy situation** when an outsider marries into the family.

Often an adult finds it hard psychologically to **'separate' from their family of origin.** However, such separation is necessary for **individual growth** and the formation of **happy relationships in adulthood**. Frequently adult children from rigid families **fail to make a life of their own**. Their original family may even encourage this. All too frequently people from rigid families cannot celebrate the success of others nor welcome 'new people' into their circle.

This means foregoing all the wonder, difference and excitement that a new person can bring into your life. **It always involves a choice**: to grow or not to grow. Focusing on the positive qualities of someone outside your original family or immediate circle not only shows maturity but will also inevitably lead to a **wider, more enriching social life.**

If you have married or partnered into such a family, refer to the persecutor, victim and rescuer triangle earlier in this Guide and **see if you can't change the role that has been assigned to you.** People only have power over us if we choose to give our power away. Also re-read the section on being assertive. **Become the person you really are**, whatever your in-law predicament.

COMMUNICATING WITH FRIENDS

The role friends play in our lives has become **significantly greater than at any other time in our history**. Today many of us live and work great distances from where we were born or grew up and are separated from our original families. The **importance of friends therefore cannot be overestimated**. The pain we feel when these relationships break down can be significant.

The happiness of the individual **relies on friendships** which form a necessary human connection. It is perfectly normal to need and want friends and depression is more prevalent among those who lack friends. They lack the intimacy and richness friends can bring into our lives.

Frequently friends **reflect similar values to us**. Yet these values are often different from the ones we grew up with; they are the values we **created for ourselves** in our adult lives.

People skills

Communication skills are **fundamental in all friendships**. The more friends and acquaintances one has, the greater are one's communication skills. Some call these **people skills**.

Like watering a plant, **we grow our friendships** (and all our relationships) by nurturing them. Friendships **need the same attention** as other relationships if they are to continue. These relationships can be delightfully non-judgemental, supportive, understanding and fun.

Sometimes a friendship can bring out the positive side that you never show in any other relationship. This may be because **the pressure of playing a 'role'** (daughter, partner or child) is removed. With a friend you are **free to be yourself** and free to change.

Of course, you are free to do this in all other relationships as well but in friendships you get to have **lots of rehearsals and discussion** about changes **as you experience them**. You can explain yourself to a friend openly, free of the fear of hurting a family member.

How people get to have friends in their lives

The answer is simple: by sharing; by revealing yourself; being attentive; **remembering what is most important to your friend** and asking them about it; putting yourself in their position; showing empathy; phoning to find out how they are; seeing the world through the eyes of your friend.

All this means **learning to accept a person** from a completely different family to your own or perhaps someone from a **completely different cultural background**. This is the way **we learn tolerance.** In turn we gain tolerance and acceptance for our own differences.

Communication skills for friendships

Friendships are made by **being considerate** which means **all the communication skills come into play:** active listening skills, questioning skills, negotiation skills, reflecting content skills, reflecting emotion skills, and editing yourself.

Friendships offer **a great opportunity to learn about yourself** because a friend can reflect back to you 'how you come across in the world'. They also allow you to practise skills in dealing with 'personal boundaries' by looking after yourself as well as your friend. They help you **develop resilience** in relation to the wider social world beyond your family.

American author Charles L. Whitfield (1993) outlined some basic principles of **how to recognise safe and unsafe people** and described the nature of personal boundaries which really defines personal rights in relationships.

A SAFE person:	An UNSAFE person:
Listens to you.	Doesn't ever listen.
Makes eye contact.	Doesn't make eye contact.
Validates you.	Doesn't validate you.
Never judges you.	Judges you often.
Knows and respects boundaries.	Blurs boundaries.
Is supportive.	Is competitive.
Is loyal.	Is disloyal, betrays you.
Is mostly positive with you.	Is mostly critical of you.
Relationship feels authentic.	Relationship feels false.

My BOUNDARIES include:	Others' BOUNDARIES include:
My awareness of my inner life.	Their awareness of their inner life.
My beliefs, thoughts, feelings, decisions, choices, experiences, my wants and needs.	Their beliefs, thoughts, feelings, decisions, choices, experiences, their wants and needs.
My behaviour.	Their behaviour.
My responsibility to make my life successful and joyful.	Their responsibility to make their life successful and joyful.

Boundaries define what you should take care of and what you allow another to take care of. Differentiating between what is yours and what belongs to another helps us to remain individual and unique. It also helps us to respect the boundaries of another and to ensure that our own boundaries **are not violated.** Dominating behaviour disallows others to be themselves and **make choices in their own best interests.** Violating another's personal boundaries leads to **low self-esteem and lack of confidence.**

No-one knows what is best for you but you. An adult takes this responsibility for themselves and allows others to **take responsibility for themselves.** Everyone can establish boundaries or draw a line in the sand that says: **'Come no further'.** This is simply **being self-protective.**

In **asserting personal boundaries** a person might say:

◆ 'I will do what is right for me.'
◆ 'I do not want your criticism, so stop now.'
◆ 'I will say what I want to say.'

Violation of another's boundary means disregarding the wishes and wants of another person. In **violating another's person boundaries** a person might say:

◆ 'Just do what I want you to do.'
◆ 'I don't care what your feelings are.'
◆ 'We'll go where I want to go.'

A person who communicates by **denying someone else** the option of negotiation is **not behaving in friendship.** They are bullying and dominant and you have the right to – and should – reject them and **protect yourself.**

Boundary problems compound communication problems when a person says:

- 'I can't say no.'
- 'I don't know what I want; you decide.'
- 'I can't be happy without a man/woman.'
- 'I don't like keeping eye-contact.'
- 'I always get involved with losers.'
- 'I worry more about others than myself.'
- 'I trust other people's opinions more than my own.'
- 'I can't ask for anything.'
- 'I just try to keep the peace.'
- 'I don't fit in with other people.'
- 'I prefer to look after others.'
- 'I don't know what I think.'
- 'I have no time to myself.'
- 'Other people's moods overly affect me.'
- 'I'm overly sensitive.'
- 'I feel emptiness all the time.'
- 'I'm always the meat in the sandwich.'
- 'I get embarrassed by 'so and so' when I'm in public.'
- 'I am overly compassionate.'
- 'My relationships feel one-sided.'
- 'I feel responsible for everyone and everything.'
- 'I can't make up my mind.'

Since such a person is not sure **where they begin and others end**, they will experience dependency problems, role confusion and low self-esteem.

COMMON CONFLICTS IN FRIENDSHIPS

Sometimes one person in a friendship feels they are **giving more than they are receiving** in terms of money, time, emotional support or attention. Good friendships allow for **unequal attention at times**, especially when one friend is going through a difficult patch. At another time it may be the other person's turn so **it all evens out in the long run**.

Abusive friendships remain unequal and are bad for both parties. Often this stems from some family role or drama being played out. Re-read the section on persecutor, victim and rescuer and make sure you or your friend is not **stuck in some role** that is stifling the friendship.

Conflict issues
Differences of opinion

One person may feel strongly about a particular matter and **seek to dominate or browbeat the friend** into agreement. Not accepting difference leads to friendship breakdown and maintains an individual's narrow worldview.

Sexuality

Generally, sexuality is **kept out of friendships**. Of course, there are always exceptions, but a sexual relationship usually obliterates friendship **because the roles change**. One is usually either lover or friend and if this becomes blurred, the friendship is likely to perish. While one can be more emotionally vulnerable, more accepted and more intimate as someone's lover, friendship requires a person to be **more hardy and resilient**. Despite needing attention to thrive, friendship **involves more objectivity than romantic attachments**.

Thoughtlessness

A friend is being thoughtless when they **override your wishes**. An example could be where one friend **dominates all decision-making** disallowing the other's ability to make choices. This could range from choosing a restaurant to deciding on a holiday destination.

It might also show up in smaller ways. For example, during a phone conversation a friend explains they are working to a deadline and can't talk for very long; the other ignores this information and blathers on.

To recognise thoughtlessness you need ask yourself only one question: '**Whose needs are being served here**?' If your wishes are not being considered, then the friendship is **psychologically abusive**. If it happens only occasionally, it might be possible to put it to down to 'a bad day'. If it happens consistently it **cannot be described as a friendship**. You either

stand up for yourself and protect yourself by **ending the friendship** or continue it which will inevitably lead to frustration, or worse, depression. (Look up the section on **'boundaries'**. If you are acting as the victim, you need to explore why **you are allowing this situation to continue**.)

'Checking in' on your friend

'Checking in' involves asking how your friend is and **actively listening to their answer**. It means looking at your friend to see if they are responding to you in conversation. It means **being mindful** of what's going on in your friend's life and not just talking about your own concerns. Essentially it is about **emotional sharing**.

Some people talk more than others so the onus might be on them to **question and elicit information** from their friend. Alternatively, the onus might be on the listener to **get active and contribute** to the conversation – otherwise the friendship is likely to be unsatisfactory and will probably dissolve over time.

The NEGATIVE FRIENDSHIP RESPONSE	The POSITIVE FRIENDSHIP RESPONSE
'You think you've got problems at work. You should have my work problems!'	'I'm interested that you think so differently about this. Tell me more.'
'You should come over tonight and work with me because I am behind.'	'I never thought of things that way?'
'No. I hate Italian food. Come on, we're eating at my French restaurant.'	'How can I help right now?'
'Your boyfriend just left you today? Well when I was with my David he said that etc etc.'	'What's happening in your life at the moment?'
'I don't want to hear about your kids, what about me?'	'How was your weekend?'
'Don't peel the potatoes that way. Let me take-over.'	'I'm sorry. I'm flat out at work right now but let's make a time to talk later tonight.'

COMMUNICATION IN THE WORKPLACE

The roles we play at work are **influenced by the way we behave** in every other situation. **We take our personality to work with us** – our social skills, our communication skills, our vulnerabilities, our strengths, our egos, our family's 'way of doing things', our morals and ethics and our sense of humour.

Although we are often told to **'leave your problems at home'**, human beings are usually **not very good at separating themselves** into compartments – so the bad mood and depression finds its way into the workplace too.

Most people are motivated in the workplace by **a number of key factors**, whether they admit it or not. These are status, recognition, money, praise and social life. Due to our **blind spots**, not many of us are aware of what motivates us. These motivators are not necessarily bad, just human. **Better communication skills** won't change our motivations but it can ameliorate them and make co-operation more likely.

Among colleagues

What is needed in the workplace is **teamwork, co-operation and good communication**. Often what exists instead are little exclusive cliques, people who can't let things go, passive aggression and a fear of confrontation. As a result, we see **poor negotiation, office politics, and bitching** – in other words **unresolved conflict**.

Since people are **reluctant to confront each other**, this all gets **explained away** as mean-spiritedness, bad manners, difficult personalities or plain old negative judgement. These situations arise not so much because of the mix of personalities but rather because of a lack of communication skills. This is why **people feel powerless and frustrated**.

It is important that each person's needs and wants in the workplace are **clearly stated**. While **negotiation skills are in serious demand**, too often people are lacking this skill. They are therefore immersed in misunderstandings.

Negotiation skills and conflict

Conflict can have a **positive role** to play in the workplace. It can end a stalemate or encourage an in-depth **analysis of a problem**. Finally, it can **lead to a resolution** that will meet the needs of both parties. **How conflict is resolved is the key**.

Good negotiation requires an appreciation that both parties' needs **must be equally addressed.** You and the other person both have different duties to perform and must meet different expectations at different times.

Ask each other in turn:

◆ What is the source (or sources) of the conflict?
◆ Is anyone else involved who should be included in the discussion?
◆ What is the history of this conflict? (Keep to the relevant facts.)
◆ What are the pressures acting on you and the other person?
◆ What is motivating this conflict and allowing it to continue?
◆ What is stopping both of you moving towards a resolution?
◆ What do you both need to happen now?
◆ Do you need any resources or assistance to make this happen?
◆ Where could you come together (even a little bit) on this problem?

Ask yourself the following questions:

◆ What would I be prepared to **'let go of'** in order to resolve this conflict?
◆ Is there a half-way position that satisfies both of us?

Draw up a plan stating that you are both **committed to do what you say.**

NEGATIVE STATEMENTS used by colleagues	POSITIVE STATEMENTS used by colleagues
'You didn't do X and I had to pick up after you.'	'We've agreed on a deadline. Can you let me know if there is a problem and we'll discuss it?'
'You always ...'	'I've noticed you did X in a different way than I would have. Can you talk me through your process?'
'You never ...'	'Have you sorted out the particular problem about C?'
'You're a joke. I don't know what it is you actually do anyway.'	'I know you must be busy, but can you pencil me in for a meeting because I have a pressing problem to discuss.'
'The boss favours John/Barbara over me.'	'I know that you are pleased with the work of John and Barbara and I'd like to get better at what I do. Have you any suggestions/feedback?'

When you are the boss
Managing in the modern way

Old fashioned styles of **authoritarian management** are becoming passé and most managers are not the owners of the business. As the boss, you are now expected to **manage in the modern way** – a co-operative way that gets the **best out of everyone** working for you. **Communication skills are paramount**.

A senior managerial role is a demanding one with many responsibilities. In addition you may have a boss above you whose expectations you have to meet. People working under your supervision look to you for praise, acknowledgement and positive responses to the tasks you set them. It is not easy to be **a friend and a boss** because sooner or later you are going to have to criticise some aspect of their work.

Exercising power fairly

As the boss, you must work for good workplace relations maintaining a **balance of authority and sociability** that is workable. Since you review people's performance and possibly make decisions in relation to their wages and working conditions, **you will be treated differently**.

Whether you like it or not, you have a **position of power** and you must find a way to exercise that power in a **civilised and fair way.** You cannot join in gossip or office politics. You have financial responsibilities on your shoulders which may involve making decisions which displease some members of staff. The aim is to be balanced and fair.

Good communication can prove **fundamental to success** in your position.

NEGATIVE RESPONSES by a boss	POSITIVE RESPONSES by a boss
'You didn't ...' 'You never ...' 'You always ...'	'I know that you have done lots of good work in the past but I want to focus on this particular problem today.'
'You will work overtime tonight and I'll hear no excuses.'	'I need you to work overtime. How are you placed for time?'
'There is nothing to negotiate.'	'Let's sit down and go through your objections. I'm happy to explain why I made that decision.'

Hints for delegating

- Let some things go unless you want to fill every minute of every day **micro managing.** (This will only have the effect of undermining your colleagues' or employees' confidence.)
- Learning to **trust others** is part of delegating and saves wasting time.
- Accept that people will **do things differently** from you. (That's just expressing their individuality!)

Remember: **modelling good communication skills** and actively encouraging such skills among your employees will be doing everyone a great service, including **the business**.

CONFLICT MANAGEMENT IN THE WORKPLACE

The **parties to a conflict** may include:

- employer and employee
- supervisor and employee
- one employee and another
- a group of employees and their employer
- an employee and a client or customer
- a trade union and an employer or employee.

Conflict in the workplace may involve issues of discrimination, prejudice or harassment. When there is conflict, management usually attempts to suppress or contain it. Sacking some people may remove the immediate problem but might also unsettle the entire work-team, causing anxiety and low morale. **The cause of the conflict must be found**. There are a variety of processes to achieve this, all of which require **good communication skills**. To be effective in communication terms, the process you choose must be seen to be **impartial, beneficial and, above all, fair.**

How to communicate better in the workplace

Making threats and **behaving in an authoritarian manner** will not create a happy workplace. It results in a **passive, uninspired workforce** and communication breakdown. Good communication needs to be demonstrated **throughout the workplace** at all levels of management.

- Be candid and self-disclosing.
- Discuss and seek feedback.
- Be approachable and visible.
- Learn to listen actively.

Check your body language

- Relaxed arms and hands **show openness**. Folded arms denote **aggression** while hands behind the head indicate **superiority**.
- **Fidgeting** distracts from your message. Maintain eye contact as gazing about the room makes you look distracted and insincere. Leaning forward **indicates genuine interest**.
- **Mirroring the body language** of another momentarily can put you 'in sync' with them.
- **Moderate your tone of voice**. Are you coming across as relaxed, aggressive or indifferent?

Develop powers of expression

- **Express yourself clearly** as this is likely to encourage similar behaviour in others.
- How many **different ways** can you say 'yes'?
- Alter perspectives by **re-framing the problem** to highlight options.

Demonstrate respect

- Show and give **mutual respect**.
- Respect others' **personal space** by maintaining an arm's length distance. Standing too close can be intimidating.
- **Being assertive** is always **better than being aggressive** because it invites responses that are authentic.

Build relationships

Building relationships through good communication in the workplace makes everyone **more productive**.

- Allow for differences.
- What seems totally appropriate to one person can seem totally inappropriate to another.
- What seems important to me may not be important to you at all.
- **Accept and value difference**. When you do, you come across as genuine.

Learn and apply communication skills

- **Learn to 'summarise'.** Pick out the key thoughts, feelings and ideas from the person you are talking to. This has the effect of making them feel **heard and valued**.

- **Try to be empathetic.** This is different from being sympathetic. Sympathy is condescending. Empathy attempts to 'go with the other person's view'. It involves putting yourself in someone else's shoes to better understand their feelings and motivations, allowing you to be open and respectful, even if you disagree with the other person.

- **Praise** and **valuing a person's contribution** in the workplace goes a long way – further than you may realise. It **promotes pride in the job**, increases commitment and reinforces a **'team spirit'**.

Dealing with an angry person

Do not correct an angry person as they will only **grow angrier**. They cannot hear you when they are angry. They are out of control and cannot think logically. They are physically and chemically in an **altered state**. You will only get into a circular conversation that goes nowhere.

To tone down an angry person, accept that they are angry. Let them get their feelings out because only then will they be capable of listening.

◆ Towards the end of their rant, reflect back **their feelings:**
  'I can tell you are really angry about this.'

◆ Reflect back **their content:**
  'You said 'this and this and that', is that right?'

◆ Push them on. **Get them to think** instead of emoting.
  'What else is upsetting you then?'

◆ Gradually their **body language** will tell you that they are calming down. They are feeling heard.

◆ You need to **engage their mind not their emotions** if you are to get an outcome. When they calm down and can focus, ask them:
  'How do you think we could do this better?' or
  'What's your solution to the problem?'

◆ Make them think it through logically and with maturity.
  'So, how do you think the other side is seeing all this?'

  Be open to change but try not to think you personally are the problem, even though the other person may have a problem with your behaviour. The **problem is the thing** you both want to tackle – **not you.**

  You are more likely to **gain respect by listening** rather than inflaming an angry attacker. Besides, there can't be an argument if one side won't participate! **Work together on better options for the future.**

THE FUTURE CHALLENGE

Now we all know that there is **more to communicating than just being a good talker** we are well on the way to better communication in all areas of our life. Remember:

◆ Try not to be too hard on yourself.
◆ Try not to become overly self-conscious.

One step at a time does it. After all, we have all learnt bad habits.

Remember we and everyone else are all doing **the best than we can** with what we have. Learning new communication skills will lead to **a big improvement in your relationships** with your family, friends and colleagues in the workplace.

You learnt to talk easily enough, now, through practice, the challenge is to communicate better!

The **publications and web links** listed on the following page will help you to **further explore** better communication skills in relation to your family, friends and colleagues.

STAY INFORMED

Publications

Beebe, Stephen A. & Masterson, John C. (2000) *Communication in Small Groups: Principles and Practices* (6th edn) Longman, New York.

Berne, E. (1964) *Games People Play*. Grove Press, New York.

Berne, Patricia H. & Savary, Louis M. (1985) *Building Self-Esteem in Children*, Continuum Publishing, New York.

Blieszner, Rosemary & Adams, Rebecca G (1992) *Adult Friendship*, Sage, Thousand Oaks, CA.

Bolton, R. (1993) *How to Assert yourself, Listen to Others and Resolve Conflict*, Simon & Schuster.

Canary, Daniel J., Cupach, William R. & Messman, Susan J. (1995) *Relationship Conflict: Conflict in Parent-Child, Friendship and Romantic Relationships*, Sage, Thousand Oaks, CA.

Cornelius, Helena & Faire, Shoshana (1989) *Everyone Can Win: How to Resolve Conflict,* Simon & Schuster, Australia.

Dangot-Simpkin, Gilda (1991) 'Making Matrix Management a Success', *Supervisory Management*, November.

DeVito, Joseph A (1989) *The Non-verbal Communication Workbook*, Waveland Press, Prospect Height, IL.

DeVito, Joseph A. (2001) *The Interpersonal Communication Book* (9th edn), Addison Wesley Longman Inc.

Faber, Adele & Mazlish, Elaine (1982) *How to Talk So Kids Will Listen and Listen So Kids Will Talk*, Avon, New York.

Fisher, Roger and Ury, William (1987) *Getting to YES. Negotiating Agreement Without Giving In,* Penguin, New York.

Goleman, Daniel (1996) *Emotional Intelligence*, Bloomsbury Publishing. UK.

Gordon, William, I. & Nevins, Randi J. (1993) *We Mean Business: Building Communication Competence in Business and Professions*, Longman, New York.

Gray, John (1992) *Men Are From Mars, Women Are From Venus*, Harper Collins, New York

Harris, Thom, MD (2004) (New Quill edn) *I'm Ok. You're OK.*, Harper Collins, New York.

Holmes, Janet (1995) *Women, Men and Politeness*, Longman, New York.

Ivy, Diana K. & Backlund, Phil (2000) *Exploring Gender-Speak: Personal Effectiveness in Gender Communication* (2nd edn) McGraw Hill, New York.

Jandt, Fred E. (1995) *Intercultural Communication,* Sage, Thousand Oaks, CA.

Mackay Hugh (1994) *Why Don't People Listen? Solving the Communication Problem,* Pan, Australia.

McKay, Matthew, Davis, Martha & Fanning, Patrick (1983) *Messages: The Communications Skills Book,* New Harbinger Publications, Oakland, CA.

McKay, Matthew & Fanning, Patrick (2000) *Self-Esteem* (3rd edn), New Harbinger Publications, Oakland, CA.

Pearson, Judy C. (1993) *Communication in the Family* (2nd edn) Harper Collins, New York.

Pease, A. (1994) *Body Language: How to Read Others' Thoughts by Their Gestures,* Harper Collins, Australia.

Robbins, Stephen P. (1989) *Training in Interpersonal Skills: Tips for Managing People at Work,* Prentice-Hall Inc., Englewood Cliffs, NJ.

Tannen, Deborah (1990) *You Just Don't Understand: Women and Men in Conversation,* Morrow, New York.

Tillett, Gregory (1999) *Resolving Conflict,* Oxford University Press, UK.

Cole, K. (1993) *Crystal Clear Communication,* Prentice Hall, New York.

Nelson Jones, R. (1991) *Human Relationship Skills* (2nd edn) Holt, Rinehart & Winston, Sydney.

Ury, William (1991) *Getting Past NO: Negotiating with Difficult People,* Business Books.

Whitford, Charles L. MD (1993) *Boundaries and Relationships: Knowing, Protecting and Enjoying the Self,* Health Communications Inc, USA.

Wilson, G. Hantz, A.M. & Hanna M.S. (1992) *Interpersonal Growth Through Communication* (3rd edn), WCB.

Websites

www.ablongman.com/html/devito/
www.queendom.com/tests/relationships/communication_skills_r_access.html
http://www.mindtools.com/page8.html
http://www.suite101.com/welcome.cfm/communications_skills
http://www.coopcomm.org/

GLOSSARY

Acknowledgement   Listening to and understanding another person. Good communication skills will make people around you feel acknowledged.

Active listening   Listening to a person without interrupting; only giving one-word responses and then asking questions about what they have said. It involves reading the other's facial expressions and focusing on them.

Assertiveness   Involves clearly stating your case and your preferred solution when an issue of concern arises and refusing to tolerate abuse.

Closed question   A closed question invites a 'yes' or 'no' answer or a single word response. 'What is your favourite sport?' or 'Did you like that film?' are both closed questions.

Communication style   The way in which each individual communicates in everyday life. In involves how a person talks, how they behave and how they react to others.

Conflict resolution   The skill set required to deal with conflict in a positive manner leading to a resolution which meets the needs of all parties.

Empathy   Involves putting yourself in someone else's shoes to better understand their feelings and motivations. It allows you to be open and respectful, even if you disagree with another person.

Family of origin   The family you were born into or were raised by.

Faux pas   A French term meaning 'false step'.

Modelling   Modelling behaviour involves setting a (negative or positive) example by acting or reacting to situations and other people in a certain way. Our families of origin model behaviour that can have a lasting affect.

Open question   The open question invites elaboration. Open questions would be 'What do you do in your spare time?' or 'What was it about the film that most interested you?'

Personal boundary   A boundary is the line where you end and another person begins. Respecting boundaries involves recognising that people are separate and different and have the right to self-determination.

Reflecting   Hearing accurately and responding appropriately to another person's statements and emotions. It involves summarising content and feelings, checking for accuracy and responding with empathy.

Self-referential   Seeing the world and other people only in relation to our own ideas and experiences.

Win/win   A highly effective, pro-active method for resolving conflict which aims to achieve a co-operative approach and fair outcomes.

INDEX